Take-Along

Travels with Baby

**Hundreds of Tips to Help During Travel with
Your Baby, Toddler, and Preschooler**

Shelly Rivoli

Travels with Baby Books, Berkeley

www.TravelswithBaby.com

ISBN 978-0-9831227-0-8

First Edition / First Printing

Important Note
This edition may contain reference to certain policies, standards, and regulations that may change over time. Always confirm critical information and seek professional advice when appropriate. Each child is unique and this book is not intended to substitute for the advice of your physician or pediatrician, or your own good judgment. Read all labels of medications and health products before use and seek professional advice if there is any confusion or indication of an emergency. Exercise common sense when using products and equipment for children, and always follow the manufacturer's instructions for use.

Special Sales
To buy books in quantity for corporate use or incentives, write to Travels with Baby, P.O. Box 7696, Berkeley, CA 94707 or email **contact@TravelswithBaby.com**

Some content in this book may have appeared previously in *Travels with Baby*, the Travels with Baby Tips blog, or in other articles written by Shelly Rivoli to which the author holds copyright. Song lyrics included are public domain.

TABLE OF CONTENTS

Acknowledgments

I want to express my deep gratitude to those who have helped make the original *Travels with Baby* a success—my family, my friends, and thousands of readers I had only dreamed would find and use the book—and in so doing helped make this Take-Along guide possible.

I would also like to thank Eugenia Araque, Davide Cis, Vanessa Forcelli, Cinzia Solari, and Camille Spanjaard for their assistance with translations in the "Babytalk" section of this book.

Additional thanks to Amy Kang for feedback on outlines and earlier drafts of this book, to Kendall Osborn, whose photo editing savvy made this cover possible; and to my copyeditor Christine LePorte, who sparked Picasso and made me look good here in spite of my "Mommy Brain."

Also, much appreciation to Polly Packard and Tim Rivoli, whose feedback and support in the final stages of this book made every difference.

Finally, I give thanks to (and for) my remarkable husband and three children who continue to enthusiastically share this adventure with me. I dedicate this book to you.

How to Get the Most from This Book

While *Travels with Baby (The Ultimate Guide* and bigger sibling to this book) helps with all aspects of planning trips before you leave home, this slim counterpart is designed to help you on the road, in the air, at the hotel, and virtually everywhere your family finds itself once you get out the door.

I can honestly tell you this is a resource I wish I'd had for myself on many occasions. So I'm as happy to know that this neatly bound copy will be in my bag the next time I travel as I am to know it will be in yours, too.

Here's how I recommend using this guide to get the most from it as you travel:

Before you go

Keep it handy, especially near your computer, as you lay your travel plans. Your customized Trip Notes begin on pg. 121, and you can simply fill in the blanks as you make decisions and reservations. That way, whenever you need to access that confirmation number or hotel address, for example, it will be much easier to flip to your trip details and see them at a glance rather than dig back through emails or boot up an electronic device (that may or may not have lost its charge).

Also, be sure to update any emergency contact information (pg. 139) and your children's current weight and height details (pg. 144) before each trip.

As you travel

Consult whichever sections you need as you travel, whether it's how to keep your tot entertained at the airport (pg. 61), determining whether or not you need a locking clip as you install a car seat in a vintage taxi (pg. 44), or consulting the Traveler's Guide to Ear Infections when you can't get to a doctor right away (pg. 106).

Also, whenever you find yourself with some lag time, on the train or perhaps by the pool, jot down a couple of details about your journey so far, including those favorite family moments, trip quotes, and invaluable "Notes for Next Time."

As you add your family's personal notes from each trip you take together, plus your child's travel art as she morphs into a budding Picasso (pg. 67)— then add a few ceremonious spills and a couple of dog-eared corners—this pocket guide will earn its rightful place as a keepsake for your family.

After your return

You may want to keep this book in your diaper bag for reference by you or your child's caregiver during daily outings. With small children, a trip across town can sometimes be as eventful as a trip overseas. Good thing you'll be prepared.

Safe journeys,

Shelly Rivoli

ON THE GO

Air Travel

At the gate, ask if one adult in your party could preboard with your car seat to have it installed before other passengers—including your child—board the aircraft. Meanwhile, you can help her burn off extra energy.

PRE-FLIGHT CHECKLIST

It can be challenging enough to pack for your trip, but just preparing for your journey through the airport—whether for your outbound flight or again for your return—can require its own special planning. In the final 24 hours before any flight with your family, use this checklist to help prepare for an air departure and help make sure you'll be ready.

- Call the airline to reconfirm your reservation as well as any special requests such as a bassinet (sky cot) or infant meals 24 hours or more in advance.

- Check in online if possible. Although you may still need to check in at the counter, this could help give you priority for your seating assignments, even if you arrive "less than early" to the airport.

- Make advance reservations for taxis, shuttles, or airport parking.

- Pack your passports where they'll be handy, or ID for adults. Don't forget your certified birth certificate to verify the age of any child traveling as a lap child or at a special reduced infant fare. [1]

---

[1] ID is not required for children traveling with adults on domestic flights in their own full-price seats.

On the Go

- Pack your paper tickets or itinerary with e-ticket info and confirmation number in an easily accessible purse or other bag.

- If only one parent or other relative is traveling abroad with the child, make sure you have any additional travel documents you will need, including a notarized consent form from the absent parent (details in Chapter 15 of *Travels with Baby*).

- Make sure you have any non-flight paperwork you will need to reach your final destination, including vouchers for shuttle services, car rentals, pre-paid hotel bookings, or airport parking (including your parking stub and location for your return!).

- Verify that FAA-approval is indicated on the label of your car seat if you are planning to use it on the aircraft (usually printed in red).

- Place a few extra diapers in the outside pocket of your checked suitcase in case you need them to be quickly accessible on arrival.

- Modify your child's Travel Kit for carry-on (see pg. 17).

- Prepare your slide-lock bag of any additional liquids you'll carry into the cabin for your child (see pg. 18).

- Make sure any additional liquids you won't need in flight are placed in your checked suitcase (e.g., extra liquid formula, baby food, larger than 3 oz. tube of diaper cream, sunblock).

- Make your game plan for getting your car seat and/or stroller through the airport (see pg. 21).

What I've learned: It's best to place all other items on the conveyor belt at security before removing your child from the stroller—not that it isn't fun ducking under ropes and chasing her through a mob of travelers while abandoning your wallet and laptop. On the other side of the scanner, collect the stroller first so you can strap your child in and park her out of the path of hurried travelers as you finish collecting your other items.

AIRPORT SECURITY READY LIST

- Make sure everyone's jacket is off, or any garments that may be considered a jacket, including zipped cardigans or sweatshirts. Store them in the side of a carry-on bag or in a backpack to have fewer loose items at the checkpoint.

- Take shoes off, including your baby's booties, in advance. Stow them in a carry-on bag or diaper bag to help keep track of them until you have finished clearing security.

On the Go

- Remove all belts with metal buckles. If you must travel with yours on, store it in your carry-on until you have made it through to your gate.

- Get wallets and keys ready to go into a bin, or place in your purse or travel bag to avoid having extra loose items to manage as you pass through the screening area.

- Place passports or IDs and boarding cards in a secure pocket, or in a side compartment of your purse or carry-on, where you can grab it when needed.

- Make sure your personal slide-lock bag of travel-size liquids is ready to access at the top of your carry-on.

- Make sure your child's slide-lock bag of travel-size liquids is ready to access at the top of your diaper bag or carry-on.

- Get additional liquids for your baby or toddler, including formula, milk, and baby food, ready to place on top of the bin and present to security (see pg. 18).

- At U.S. airports, head for the green "Family Lane" at security if it is open. You may be able to bypass a lengthy line of travelers, and your screener won't be so likely to blink when you pull out the baby food and bottles.

PREPARING LIQUIDS FOR CARRY-ON

Your Child's Travel Kit:

In addition to your own quart-size plastic bag of 3 oz. or smaller individual liquid containers (100ml for EU airports), you may also bring one onboard for your child, even when she flies as a lap child. Here are my suggestions from *Travels with Baby* for a modified Travel Kit you can carry into the cabin:

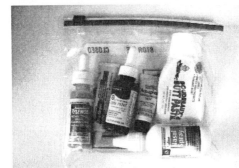

Travel kit for carry-on with 3 oz. liquid restrictions:

- Infants' Tylenol, 1 fl. oz.
- Infants' gas relief drops, 1 fl. oz.
- Small tube of diaper cream, 2 oz.
- Small tube of teething gel, .33 oz.
- Sample tube of moisturizing cream (from doctor's office), .25 oz.
- Saline nasal spray, 1.5 fl. oz.

On the Go

Baby Bottles, Formula, Milk, and Baby Food:

- As long as you are clearing security *with* your baby or toddler, you may also bring onboard liquid infant formula, expressed breast milk, regular milk, and baby food in what the security officer deems to be "reasonable quantities" for your itinerary.
- Bottled water that is not mixed with powdered formula is not permitted past the security point.
- Keep all prepared bottles, milk, and baby food where they will be easy to pull out and set on top of items in your bin to present at security.
- A gallon-size slide-lock bag works well for keeping these extra liquid items together and will contain any leaks in flight.
- Remember to put any additional liquid formula, boxed milk, or baby food you won't need in flight into a checked bag.

In the Event of a Ban on Liquids or Gels:

Even when a complete liquid ban is in effect, parents traveling with a baby or toddler have still been allowed to bring a reasonable amount of infant formula, expressed breast milk, and/or liquid baby foods into the cabin, though security will take a very close look at your flight itinerary to decide how much is "reasonable" for your journey. You can call your airline if you have specific questions, but if lines are busy, try www.TSA.gov/travelers.

WHAT TO DOUBLE CHECK AT CHECK-IN

In spite of your best efforts to plan ahead and reserve in advance, it never hurts to reconfirm these points at check-in. Seats can be reassigned at the last minute for flights, and families can even be separated with surprising frequency.

- If your child is flying in a paid seat, do you have appropriate seat assignments for using his car seat if desired (more on pg. 23)?

- Can you gate-check your stroller and/or car seat when you board the aircraft?

- Will you have the bassinet that you reserved for your long-haul flight, and the appropriate seats for using the bassinet? Even "reserved" bassinets are issued on a first-come first-checked in basis.

WHAT TO ASK AT THE GATE

- Request "gate check tags" for your stroller and/or car seat. These are separate luggage tags provided by the airline that easily identify your gate-checked items for baggage handlers on both ends of your flight.

- Ask whether or not there will be family preboarding for your flight and where your family should line up.

On the Go

- If you are a frequent flyer member, ask whether or not your member status allows you to board before the family preboarders.

- If you'd prefer to wait to board while your child burns off energy, ask if one adult in your party could preboard with your car seat to have it installed before other passengers—including your child—board the aircraft.

WHEN AND WHY TO GATE-CHECK GEAR

At time of writing virtually all major airlines, including those that charge hefty fees for checked suitcases, still allow travelers to check car seats and strollers for free. In most cases, you will have the option to either check these items at the front counter or bring them with you to check at the gate. While there is certainly the temptation to offload as much as possible as soon as possible at the airport, here are a few reasons you might want to bring yours to the gate instead.

- **Car seat** – Even if you are not planning to use your child's car seat on the airplane, you may not want to subject its thin plastic shell to the rigors of the airport baggage system and falling 50 lb. suitcases. Your car seat is also more likely to meet you on the other end if it is checked at the gate of your actual airplane. And finally, in the event that there is an open seat remaining on your flight, your lap child will be able to use it for all phases of your flight (not so for children under 24 months without a car seat).

- **Stroller** – With it, you may be able to move your child more quickly through the airport, and without getting bumped by rolling suitcases. During a layover, your gate-checked stroller might also assist with a gate change, help with napping, or provide a seat for your child at a restaurant or crowded gate. At baggage claim, it may also help keep your child safely out of the way while you retrieve your suitcases and dodge others. If you're considering wearing your baby in an Ergo or similar child carrier, remember that you may be asked to remove your baby from it and it from you in your final moments at security. It may be easier to "reassemble" on the other side of the scanner with a travel stroller. On the down side, you will have to look for elevators as you move through the airport, and your child won't get as much exercise before the flight.

GETTING YOUR CAR SEAT TO THE GATE

If you don't have the benefit of the great products or gear recommended in *Travels with Baby* to help get your car seat to the gate, here a few ways that may still ease your burden on the fly:

On the Go

Toddler car seat + adult – Lengthen the straps of toddler car seats and try wearing them over your shoulders like a backpack with the car seat behind you. This works best with larger car seats and smaller-shouldered adults.

Toddler car seat + travel stroller – With umbrella-style "hook" handles on your stroller, turn the car seat toward the back of your stroller and run the handles through the straps. Remember, if the car seat weighs more than your stroller, remove it first or the stroller will tip when you pull your child out.

Infant car seat + travel stroller – With infant carrier car seats that don't attach to the stroller, put the carrying handle in the back position and turn the car seat toward the stroller and hang the car seat from the handle.

Infant car seat + carry-on suitcase – Extend the handle of your carry-on suitcase to the fully extended position, then turn your infant carrier car seat toward it and hang it from the suitcase handle on the side that will face up as you lean and roll the suitcase.

What I've learned: Less is not always more when you are flying with a toddler and a preschooler. A sudden gate change can turn a calm and controlled wait into a mad dash for another terminal through a hurried crowd armed with rolling suitcases—not the best time to have left the travel stroller at home and have your small children lugging their own backpacks.

INSTALLING CAR SEATS ON AIRPLANES

Car seats are installed on airplanes just as they are in automobiles using a lap safety belt. Your car seat must be FAA-approved for air travel[2], which is usually indicated on a label found on its side. Booster seats that require a shoulder safety belt are not approved for use in airplanes. Here are a few pointers that may help with your installation.

- **Car seats must be installed in the window seat position, or in the middle of a center row** of seats on large aircraft, where they will not block other passengers exiting their seats.

- **When flying with the Sit 'N' Stroll,** request a seatbelt extension from a flight attendant as you board the aircraft.

- **Lift arm rests to help create extra space** for your child's car seat and give your hands that extra space needed to buckle it in place.

- **In seats with fixed arm rests, turn the seatbelt buckle over** so that it lifts to open away from the arm rest. Otherwise, it may be difficult to open the buckle after landing.

- **When flying with an antsy toddler,** consider installing a convertible car seat in the rear-facing position to help keep him from kicking the

[2] Or noted by similar authority in other countries and also labeled on the car seat.

forward passenger's seat. You'll be surprised how he settles in to his seat with legs "criss-cross applesauce."

EAR PRESSURE, PAIN, AND RELIEF

It may be easier sometimes than others to coordinate a feeding with the timing of your flight or its landing. While your child doesn't necessarily have to be awake—or drinking liquid—in order for her ears to adjust, it is a comfort to any parent to know that painful pressure is not building up. Watch your child carefully for signs of discomfort, especially during the descent, and just remember that any way you can get the jaw moving can help ears adjust:

- Breastfeeding
- Bottle feeding
- Cup feeding
- Sucking pacifiers
- Chewing a teething toy
- Gnawing on a teething biscuit
- Snacking
- Licking a lollipop
- Pretend yawning
- Talking
- Laughing (give a tickle!)
- Singing

More tips for helping ears adjust

- Make sure you have a bottle, cup, or snack ready *before* your airplane begins its descent, ear pressure starts to build, and the seatbelt signs prevent you from getting helpful items from the overhead bin or a flight attendant.

- When babies are bored with the bottle or are quite satisfied from nursing, try cup feeding with a little cold water in the cap of a baby bottle.

What I've learned: When flying with a toddler or preschooler who is already nervous about the changes she feels in her ears, avoid using the expression "your ears are popping"!

BREASTFEEDING ON AIRPLANES

- **Avoid aisle seats for fewer distractions to your child and greater privacy.** Window seats are most ideal when not flying with a car seat, which gets priority window seating, of course.

- **Abandon the bulkhead row.** If the traffic to the lavatory and/or noise from the galley is too disruptive, seats in the rear of the airplane are usually the last to be assigned, so there may still be some vacancies if you need to take a stroll mid-flight. On overnight flights, you might want to stake one out as soon as possible to keep as a backup for your family.

- **Use the fan.** The individual fan above you can be useful in three ways: 1) It can create a little white noise over your neighbors to minimize distractions, 2) It can help keep baby cool as she rests against you during a stuffy, warm flight, and 3) It can help encourage little eyes to stay closed when they might be tempted to continue taking in all the new surroundings rather than focusing on mealtime.

- **Lift and drape.** With your moderately loose shirt raised up for access, you can drape the fabric gently over your child's cheek for adequate modesty without having to cover her head or face. If she suddenly pulls away, you've got it covered.

- **Go to the loo.** While restrooms are the last place most of us would want to feed our children, there are some times during travel when it may simply be the most practical solution. One mom trapped on a 12-hour flight with her hungry infant tried everything she could think of to get her highly distractible baby to feed at her seat. In the end, it was only in the white-noise-infused lavatory, devoid of well-meaning passengers trying to amuse the crying baby, that she was able, at last, to fill her baby's tummy.

See more tips in Breastfeeding on the Go, pg. 90.

SOOTHING FUSSY BABIES ON AIRPLANES

- **Do your best to relax and show your baby you are calm and confident** in the strange new environment of the aircraft. If you are nervous about your baby's ears adjusting or simply sensitive to her cries, your child may sense your anxiety and react to that as much as anything else.

- **If you haven't already, read over the tips for helping ears** adjust in flight (pg. 24).

- **For babies who are not yet ready to sleep,** but are not sure about the new setting, play "Uppa Baby Elevator" by raising them up to peek over your seat back at the passengers behind you, then down, then up. Repeat as necessary. It's not only a great upper-body workout for you, but a strategic method for winning over the other passengers before she gets tired.

- **For overtired and sensitive babies,** minimize outside stimulation by turning off reading lights and at-seat TVs, closing window shades, and seating your child as far from the many new faces as possible. (See other tips for helping children sleep in flight on pg. 31)

- **Help rule out gas pain and pressure** that may be worsened by rapid elevation gains by enabling your baby to move and stretch at your seats. Take little walkers and cruisers for a short jaunt up and down the aisle. Consider giving the appropriate dose of simethicone gas relief drops (Mylicon or other) from your child's Travel Kit.

- **Help her "cool her jets."** Airplane cabins can be stuffy places, and if she's been fussing for long, she may have worked up a sweat and could be overheated. Try removing a layer of clothing and offering water, even in an open-top cup from the flight attendant (which we've found is always more interesting than the familiar bottle or sippy cup).

- **Take a trip to the lavatory and strip her down** to a fresh, dry diaper (some babies will be happy just to be naked!). Check for a rogue hair or clothing tag that may be irritating her skin. If there's any chance the clothing may be binding or rubbing her the wrong way, try a new outfit.

MANAGING TODDLERS ON AIRPLANES

Here are tips and solutions for the five most common complaints I hear concerning the delicate art of flying with toddlers.

1. **Escaping seatbelts** – Airplane seatbelts alone are easily unbuckled by tots. Establish the importance of seatbelts or the safety harness up front with your child, and that everyone must

wear their seatbelts in their seats on the airplane—even you. If this is likely to be an issue with your child, consider using his car seat onboard, which in most cases will be more of a challenge to unbuckle. If you are not traveling with a car seat, or are using the CARES flight safety harness instead, try discreetly turning the seat buckle over as you fasten it, so that it opens against your child instead of easily lifting out and away.

2. **Kicking seats** – If your child is a "kicking risk," install his car seat rear-facing so that the only seat he'll be able to kick is his own. Since he'll be able to recline more in this position, it may also help him get a little more rest during the flight— and keep toys in his lap. Longer legs fold a la "criss-cross apple sauce." This can also be helpful for children obsessed with the in-seat TV and buttons, or constantly folding and unfolding the tray table.

3. **Lack of physical freedom** – Help keep very active toddlers in motion without leaving their seats by encouraging activities that can keep their hands busy even while the rest of them must remain seated. Ask your flight attendant for extra napkins and start making origami hats, and get out those crayons, Legos, or plastic dinosaurs who are in dire need of a new napkin wardrobe (see more ideas on pg. 32).

4.   **Hyperactivity** – Avoid giving your child juice—
     or at least full-strength fruit juices in flight—and
     avoid high-sugar snacks (28 grams of sugar in
     fruit juice can be a lot for a 28 lb. person).
     Without enough room to burn off the sugar, it
     gives little passengers an unfair disadvantage. If
     it's too late, try to help stabilize the sugar with a
     protein snack before the post-sugar crash.

5.   **Boredom** – Help him "think outside the aircraft"
     by writing a letter or postcard to a friend about
     the adventure so far. What have been his
     favorite or most exciting parts of the trip? Or
     what does he hope to do and see while away?

What I've learned: A five-hour flight with an overtired toddler is not the time to find out that, while it's commonly believed that the antihistamine Benadryl may be used to help children sleep on airplanes, it also has the opposite effect in some children. Mine included. A better bet may be a "sleepytime snack" as described on pg. 83.

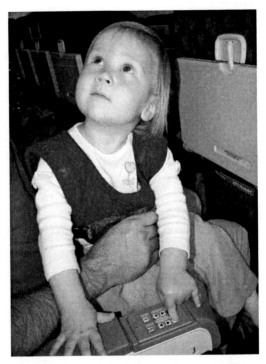

On long flights, you may be happy to let your toddler start pushing your buttons.

HELPING CHILDREN SLEEP ON AIRPLANES

- **Surrender your seats on the bulkhead row.** For some children this location, with lavatory traffic, possible galley noise, or even projected video, will simply be too stimulating for sleep. If so, look for empty seats toward the rear of the

31

aircraft or ask passengers if they might be willing to trade.

- **Install your toddler's convertible car seat rear-facing,** even if he rides forward-facing at home. This will allow you to recline the car seat and create a more restful spot to snooze without the drooping head.

- **Go for a walk.** Sometimes children don't realize how tired they've become just sitting in one place. Taking a brief stroll around the aircraft may help them make peace with settling in for a snooze.

- **Get ready for bed.** Even though the interior of the airplane is vastly different from home, familiar rituals like brushing teeth and putting on pajamas can help put the wheels of bedtime in motion.

- **Create a "blanket tent."** Whether you're competing with neighboring reading lights, combating the drying effects of air vents, or simply trying to block out other distractions on the plane, a blanket may do the trick. Take an airline-issue blanket and tuck one corner into the top of the airplane tray table in front of you (closed position) and create a canopy over your child's seat or wrap the blanket around your side as a barrier. On some airplanes, headrests may also help create your custom tent.

Driving & Road Trips

Decreasing the degree of recline of rear-facing car seats helps babies take in the scenery for longer periods without straining their necks. An attached bottle with water helps keep them entertained as well as hydrated.

TIPS FOR A HAPPIER BACKSEAT BABY

- **Keep him company.** Unless he's napping, have a fellow passenger ride beside the baby to play simple games, smile, and assure him he's not alone in this journey.

- **If your baby is old enough and has sufficient control of his head and neck muscles, decrease the recline of the car seat** from 45 degrees up to 30 degrees to help keep him from straining his neck muscles to look around the car (more on pg. 46).

- **Give her a bottle with water** to help keep her entertained and hydrated, especially if you are running the heat or AC much on your trip. This will also help her ears adjust if they may be lagging after a steep mountain ascent or descent.

- **Add some cush for her tush.** Since many car seats offer little more than a thin cover over a hard plastic shell, baby buns can grow weary after too much time on the road. Fold a sweater or small blanket, or place an extra diaper beneath her to make things more comfy.

- **Pull over and take a break.** Everyone needs to stretch their legs, even those who can't yet walk. Lay a blanket on the backseat or park lawn and let your little one stretch and sprawl at least once every 2 hours while awake. Remember physical movement may also help move along digestion and ease related discomforts.

- **Add head support on winding roads**. A baby's head can loll back and forth a surprising amount while driving through a curvy mountain pass and make it nearly impossible for some children to sleep—or stay asleep—during the drive. Roll up a blanket, towel, or jacket to add support to both sides.

Even babies who can't yet walk need a chance to stretch their legs during lengthy road trips.

On the Go

QUALITY CAR TIME WITH YOUNG KIDS

- With your toddler or preschooler, talk about your destination and help your child visualize what you will do, where you will stay, and who you will visit.

- Take turns telling a continuing story aloud.

- Decide which three things you would most like to do before you get home from your trip.

- Decide which three things you would most like to do when you get home *after* your trip.

- Practice counting in Spanish, French, or any language you prefer.

- Sing a simple song together as a round or, if you're up to it, sing it in harmony.

- Talk about your child's first week at home.

- Share your favorite memory of one of your child's grandparents.

- Share a memory from one of your early trips as a child (camping, car trip, airplane ride, train ride…).

- With preschoolers, this is a great time to discuss things they will be able to do to be helpful or thoughtful while visiting a relative's home.

- Practice memorizing a simple poem or favorite rhyming children's story together (see Easy Songs to Sing, pg. 55).

FAVORITE FAIR-WEATHER ROAD STOPS

Much depends on where your drive takes you, but here are some good bets for breaking up the drive with babies and young children:

- **State Parks** – Whether at the beach or in the woods, you're pretty much guaranteed to find restrooms, picnic tables, and some sort of nature trail.

- **Rest Areas** – To the traveling adult it may look like little more than a parking lot and restrooms. To your wee adventurer, however, it may be as thrilling a picnic site as any, complete with a sprawling lawn with dandelion wishes waiting to be made.

- **Scenic Turnouts** – Plan ahead to pause for a picnic at one when you'll be traveling a winding mountain pass or along cliffs above the sea where other stops and services may be few and far between.

- **Rivers, Creeks, and Ponds** – Ducks to feed? Rocks to throw? Water to splash and cool off in? Don't forget to wave at passing boats or catch mudskippers in a cup.

- **Outdoor Fountains** – Enjoy some cool drinks together as you watch your cruiser circle the town square fountain or your toddler run laps tirelessly around the focal point of a park.

On the Go

HOW TO MAKE THE MOST OF ROAD STOPS

- Blow bubbles—you can always buy some at a drug store en route.

- Make dandelion wishes where available.

- Chase a rubber ball.

- Make new friends at the local park.

- Feed the birds.

- Buy ice cream cones or popsicles.

- Practice doing somersaults.

- Collect leaves, pine cones, or wildflowers.

BEST-BET RAINY DAY ROAD STOPS

In fair weather, it's much easier to find suitable stops where kids can run around and get a much-needed break from the backseat. If your road trip runs into rain or snow, try these foolproof pitstops with young children. You may also find some helpful ideas in "Entertainment to Go," beginning on pg. 53.

- **Local library** – Brimming with books, restrooms (most with a changing table), drinking fountains, and occasionally interesting art displays. Most towns have signs pointing you in the right direction to make it easy as well.

- **Pet store** – Stretch your legs and feast your eyes on things that slither and gobble up flies. Birds and fish are sure to please, plus furry rodents who dream of cheese.

- **The McRestaurant** – While it may not top your list of travel destinations, a dry and heated climbing maze of tubes and slides is hard to beat for a rainy-day roadstop with energetic children—especially for the cost of a cup of coffee.

- **One dollar stores** – Chock full of toys and art supplies, coloring books, and often snacks, and found in numerous strip malls across the continent. What better place to let your child choose a souvenir and snack for the next stretch of road?

- **Shopping mall** – Not only does it provide climate-controlled pedestrian strolling and restrooms, but some also come equipped with a children's play area, food court, and in a pinch…a toy store.

ADJUSTING A RENTAL CAR SEAT

If you have rented or borrowed a car seat, it may be easiest to adjust it to fit your child properly *before* you install it in the car (except for certain no-thread harness models). Place your child in the car seat to check which shoulder harness slots are the best fit, keeping in mind that:

On the Go

- **Rear-facing car seat shoulder straps** should be at or just below the shoulders.
- **Forward-facing car seat shoulder straps** should be at or just above the shoulders.
- **Chest clips always go at armpit-level.**

The car seat manual should be stored in the back of the car seat or underneath its cover (typical of Britax models) if you need it for reference.

CAR SEAT INSTALLATION TIPS

Whether you're installing a car seat you've never seen before, or you're using your own in a completely different vehicle, these tips may help.

1. The diagram on the side of the car seat should show the proper safety belt or LATCH path. For help finding LATCH anchors, see pg. 41.
2. If you are not familiar with the type of seatbelt you find in an older vehicle, identify it in the section beginning on pg. 42.
3. Once the seat is buckled in, apply your weight with your knee, if possible, to help press it into the vehicle seat, and tighten the belt.
4. If the car seat moves more than 1 inch in any direction, try applying more weight and further tightening the belt.
5. If you aren't sure if you need a locking clip to keep the seat secure, see pg. 44.

LOCATING LATCH ANCHORS

LATCH anchors are standard in vehicles model year 2003 and newer, though they are easier to find in some backseats than others. Some vehicles have LATCH anchors in the outermost rear seating positions only, and not in a center seat position, which may only have a safety belt. If the LATCH anchors are not visible at first glance, look for small dots or other indications of where they might be on the lower seat back, and feel just inside of where the seatbelts are positioned.

WHERE TO ANCHOR THE TETHER

If you've kept your child riding rear-facing thus far, you may be new to the "top tether." Tethers are generally used with forward-facing car seats only, and connect to the car's anchor points after the car seat has been installed with the seatbelt or LATCH. If the location of the tether anchor isn't completely obvious in your rental or relative's car, check these locations:

- The floor below the seat
- The rear window "shelf" of sedans
- On the floor of the cargo bay in minivans or SUVs
- In the ceiling of SUVs and station wagons.

On the Go

If you are still scratching your head, check the glove box for the vehicle owner's manual, or chase down the guy who rented the car to you. If he can't find it either, there may be a free upgrade in your future.

TYPES OF SEATBELTS YOU MAY ENCOUNTER

While you may use LATCH anchors for your car seat at home, you may need to use seatbelts to install your car seat at times as you travel. For help installing your car seats with seatbelts, find the belt type in the following list.

- **Manually adjusting lap-only belt** – Similar to seatbelts found on airplanes, you can pull the free end of the seatbelt to shorten it, and the latch plate locks to hold the seatbelt in place once adjusted.
- **Automatic locking retractor (ALR)** – This belt pulls out from the retractor, and then locks in place at the specified length. It cannot be lengthened from this point until it has been completely retracted again. Once your car seat is in place, give a hard tug to lock the buckled seatbelt in place.
- **Emergency locking retractor (ELR)** – This seatbelt moves freely in and out of the retractor

and only locks in place when the vehicle comes to a sudden stop. These belts are not recommended for use with car seats unless a vehicle manufacturer's belt-shortening clip is provided. ELRs were discontinued after 1995. Check seatbelt near buckle in case it is labeled as an ELR/ALR (see next point). If not, use a manually adjusted center position lap belt instead if possible.

- **Switchable ELR/ALR combination retractor** – Most of these belts will move freely for normal, adult use, like an ELR. But they can switch to ALR mode by pulling the belt all of the way out of the retractor (after you have buckled the seatbelt through the car seat), then allowing the belt to retract to fit the car seat. There may be a label with instructions on switching modes affixed to the seatbelt. Make sure you switch to the ALR mode when installing your car seat.

- **Continuous loop lap/shoulder belt** – One belt passes through the latch plate of this belt, forming both the lap and shoulder segments. If the latch plate locks in place once buckled, holding the car seat in place with the lap belt portion, no locking clip is needed. If the latch plate slides freely along the belt, you will need to use your locking clip (see pg. 44).

- **Automatic seatbelts** – These should never be used with car seats. If the lap belt portion is not automated, and you can unhook the automatic shoulder belt, that may be wisest—but check to see if the lap belt is an ELR, in which case a manufacturer's belt shortening clip should be used. Most automatic seatbelts are in the front seats and can be avoided by simply using the backseat.

HOW AND WHEN TO USE A LOCKING CLIP

Some vehicles, especially those model year 1995 and older, may require a locking clip for secure installation of car seats with continuous loop safety belts (see pg. 43). Locking clips are the H-shaped metal clips that still come packaged with most child safety seats, and are usually stored under the base or on the back of the car seat.

See your car seat manual for specifics on using a locking clip with your model. In general:

* The clip is used to fasten together the lap and shoulder portions of a shoulder seatbelt where the strap slides freely through the latch plate.

* The clip should be used just above the latch plate to prevent the seatbelt from sliding through it.

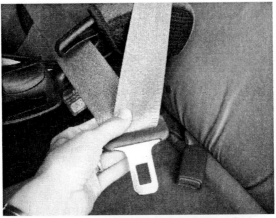

A continuous loop seatbelt before the locking clip...

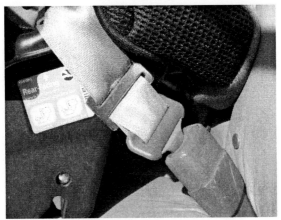

...and after the locking clip has been used.

On the Go

COMBATING CARSICKNESS

Carsickness can sneak up on any member of the family, but children—trapped in the backseats and oftentimes seated lower than the car windows—can be especially prone to the condition. After a good dose of fresh air and touching down on terra firma, consider these points before returning to the road:

- **Decrease the recline** of rear-facing car seats for babies once they can support their heads well. The American Academy of Pediatrics suggests a 33 to 15 degree recline for older babies and toddlers riding in rear-facing seats.
- **Move your child to the center seat position** if he will be able to better see out the front window as you travel.
- **Avoid the blood sugar blues** by keeping meals balanced and as timely as possible. Back-up snacks should be low in sugar (beware of fruit juice) to avoid sugar spikes and the woes that follow.
- **Stay hydrated.**
- **Keep fresh air circulating** through the car either through open windows or vent settings.
- **Avoid entertainment through toys or books that cause your child to look down**. Instead, help encourage your child to look up and out the windows by playing games like "Red Car! Blue Car!" and singing songs, or listening to books on tape (more ideas beginning on pg. 53).

Diapers & Potty Training

Never a diaper changing station where you need one?
Take advantage of the tailgate of your car or rental car.

On the Go

CHANGING DIAPERS ON THE GO

- **Stash a few diapers, a travel-size pack of baby wipes, and antibacterial hand wipes in your glove box** to create a quick-change diapering station for infants who need frequent service.

- **Keep a gallon-size slide-lock bag** with you for stink-proof stowage of dirty diapers when garbage cans aren't readily available.

- **Be sure to place a clean diaper below your baby** before removing the soiled one—just in case.

- **Bring your child carrier, sling, or stroller** with you into restrooms when possible to give you a place to put your baby while you wash your hands, possibly rinse out soiled clothing if needed, and use the restroom yourself, of course.

- **Take advantage of the tailgate** of your car if you are driving or have rented a minivan, SUV, crossover, or station wagon.

- **Take advantage of your reclining travel stroller** to change your infant in restrooms without changing tables.

CHANGING DIAPERS ON AIRPLANES

- On *most* **airplanes with 3 or more lavatories,** at least one will be equipped with a diaper changing table that folds down from the wall. Often these are in the rear of the aircraft, but ask a flight attendant if you have trouble locating it.

- **If there isn't a changing table onboard,** try to time your diaper change with your neighbor's visit to the lavatory if possible. You won't risk offending them and you'll hopefully have more room to maneuver.

- **If you have seats on the bulkhead row,** consider using the floor space. Although you'll have very little privacy, you'll have more room to work and less risk of your baby rolling off the seats or a lavatory toilet.

- **When your toddler is too big** for airplane lavatory changing tables, have him stand on the toilet seat instead to do a "standing quick change" (see pg. 50).

- **Use a plastic bag to seal up stinky diapers** before depositing them in the lavatory trash (thank you!). In a pinch you can swipe an airsickness bag from the seat pocket in front of you.

- **Remember flight attendants are in the food service business** and cannot legally dispose of a diaper for you, so make your own arrangements.

On the Go

THE "STANDING QUICK CHANGE"

Looking at your sweet, delicate infant now, it may be hard to imagine the time will come when he becomes a master of the Diaper Defense Arts. Airplanes and cars are no place for him to practice these impressive—and potentially disastrous—skills. When changes must be made regardless, remember toddlers usually seem much more content when standing on their own two feet—even during a diaper change. Try this:

- Have your kung-fu warrior stand on the lavatory toilet lid facing the wall, or in the doorway of your car or van.

- Let him hold onto the lavatory wall or the vehicle seats for support, which will keep his hands busy in a *helpful* manner.

- Pull his pants down and leave at the ankles to inhibit the climbing instinct and kicking reflex.

- Remove the diaper, wipe, and replace.

- Return pants to their upright position.

- Wash hands or use antibacterial hand wipes.

- Give a high five.

What I've learned: *When travel delays find you running short on diapers, lay a few folded paper towels in the diaper and use the diaper itself as a cover. It's not ideal, but it can definitely help stretch your diapers in a pinch.*

TIPS FOR TRAVEL WITH POTTY TRAINEES

- At international and larger airports, check the directory or ask if there is a family restroom or separate handicap facility available, where the usual noise of several hand dryers and auto-flushing toilets won't intimidate and overwhelm young children.

- Hold your hand over auto flush sensors until your child is done to avoid untimely and terrifying flushes.

- Keep a small baggie in your purse or daypack with tasty rewards to help overcome anxiety about "trying" in strange places—even if you've already moved well past this point of training back at home.

- Remember that irregularity is common in travelers of all ages, and may disrupt your potty trainee's routine at times, whether or not the reason why is clear to your child. Be patient and help your child cope with the issue. (See tips for managing regularity issues on pg. 103.)

- Rather than just any old plastic bag you come upon, keep a gallon size slide-lock plastic bag (perhaps one you had packed in your suitcase) in your purse or day bag to contain messy clothes while you're out and about. They will help contain odors better than plastic shopping bags, and are easy to add to if necessary.

On the Go

- When traveling abroad with a potty trainee, where public restrooms may be far less common—or desirable—plan lunch or snack breaks at larger restaurants with their own restrooms (and attendants).

- When all else fails, in any nation, head to the Golden Arches. We've come to believe they are golden for good reason.

What I've learned: Before passing through the fortified gates of Wildlife Safari in your family car—which you will not be permitted to stop nor exit during the 1-hour driving tour, do not ask your preschooler if she needs to use the potty. Just take her. Even with a training potty in the car, it can be a long and bumpy ride...

Entertainment to Go

At the airport, buy a few postcards and let your child send greetings to family and friends, even if this means loving scribbles or doodles by her own hand.

On the Go

GAMES FOR FAMILY CAR TRIPS

Many traditional family road trip games are a bit beyond toddlers and preschoolers. Here are some variations and new inspirations that have worked for us.

- Play "Minivan!" or other vehicle of your choice by being the first to shout out the car type when spotted on the road.

- "I spy with my little eye…" something in this car… With young children it's usually best not to choose from the passing scenery!

- Keep a running count of each "Red car!" you see on the way. When your children are old enough, you can choose different colors and keep score.

- Be "Animal Ambassadors" by appointing a Vice President in charge of horses and a Commander in Chief of Cows to greet the animals in their languages each time you pass them.

- "Make That Noise," taking turns each time a passenger names a sound; e.g., the ocean, a pig, trumpet, purring cat, big truck, flushing toilet, etc.

- "I'm going on a picnic and I'm brining lots of…" You can also take turns filling in the blanks with all sorts of variations, including, "I'm going on vacation and I'm packing my own…"

EASY SONGS TO SING IN THE CAR

Dare yourselves to take a break from the iPod, MP3 player, CDs, and radio, and make your own music. Not only is singing these songs with children a time-honored tradition (note the earliest years of known publication on these old, familiar tunes), but at some point your child may frown upon your melodious refrains in the car altogether. Sing while you can!

Frère Jacques (1811)

Are you sleeping? Are you sleeping?

Brother John? Brother John?

Morning bells are ringing,

Morning bells are ringing,

Ding, dang, dong…Ding, dang, dong.

Frère Jacques, Frère Jacques,

Dormez vous? Dormez vous?

Sonnez les matines,

Sonnez les matines!

Din, din, don…Din, din, don.

On the Go

London Bridge Is Falling Down (1744)

London Bridge is falling down,
Falling down, falling down.
London Bridge is falling down,
My fair lady.

Build it up with iron bars,
Iron bars, iron bars,
Build it up with iron bars,
My fair lady.

Iron bars will bend and break,
Bend and break, bend and break,
Iron bars will bend and break,
My fair lady.

Build it up with gold and silver,
Gold and silver, gold and silver,
Build it up with gold and silver,
My fair lady.

Baa, Baa, Black Sheep (1765)

Baa, baa, black sheep, have you any wool?

Yes, sir, yes, sir,

Three bags full:

One for my master and one for my dame,

And one for the little boy that lives in the lane.

Baa, baa, black sheep, have you any wool?

Yes, sir, yes, sir,

Three bags full.

Oh Where, Oh Where Has My Little Dog Gone? (1864)

Oh, where, oh, where has my little dog gone?

Oh, where, oh, where can he be?

With his ears cut short and his tail cut long,

Oh, where, oh, where can he be?

On the Go

The Farmer in the Dell (1883)

The farmer in the dell, the famer in the dell,

Heigh oh, the derry-oh,

The farmer in the dell.

Verse 2: The farmer takes a wife

Verse 3: The wife takes a nurse

Verse 4: The nurse takes a child

Verse 5: The child takes a dog

Verse 6: The dog takes a cat

Verse 7: The cat takes a rat

Verse 8: The rat takes the cheese

Verse 9: The cheese stands alone

Polly Wolly Doodle (1885)

Oh, I went down South

For to see my Sal,

Sing Polly wolly doodle all the day

My Sal, she is a spunky gal

Sing Polly wolly doodle all the day.

Entertainment to Go

Chorus:

Fare thee well, fare thee well,

Fare thee well my fairy fay,

For I'm going to Lou'siana for to see my Susyanna,

Sing Polly wolly doodle all the day.

Oh, my Sal, she is a maiden fair,

Sing Polly wolly doodle all the day,

With curly eyes and laughing hair,

Sing Polly wolly doodle all the day. (chorus)

Behind the barn, down on my knees,

Sing Polly wolly doodle all the day,

I thought I heard a chicken sneeze,

Sing Polly wolly doodle all the day. (chorus)

He sneezed so hard with the whooping cough,

Sing Polly wolly doodle all the day,

He sneezed his head and the tail right off,

Sing Polly wolly doodle all the day. (chorus)

On the Go

Oh, a grasshopper sittin' on a railroad track,
Sing Polly wolly doodle all the day,
A-pickin' his teeth with a carpet tack,
Sing Polly wolly doodle all the day. (chorus)

Oh, I went to bed, but it wasn't any use,
Sing Polly wolly doodle all the day,
My feet stuck out like a chicken roost,
Sing Polly wolly doodle all the day. (chorus)

Alouette (1879)

Alouette, gentille Alouette,
Alouette, je te plumerai.
Je te plumerai la tête,
Je te plumerai la tête.
Et la tête,
Et la tête,
O-O-O-OH!
Alouette, gentille Alouette,
Allouette, je te plumerai.

ENTERTAINING TOTS IN THE AIRPORT

- Fill water bottles for your flight at a drinking fountain.
- Ride the escalators.
- Ride the elevators.
- Play "I see a blue coat, I see a black coat" (or some version of "I spy with my little eye").
- Count backpacks.
- Have a picnic at a vacated gate.
- Watch the airplanes taxi and take off.
- Watch the trucks bringing suitcases to the airplanes. Watch for your own.
- Watch the airplanes descend and applaud the smoothest landings.
- Befriend airline personnel awaiting your flight with questions like, "How many times have you flown on an airplane?" and "Have you ever seen Santa Claus up there?"
- Do the Hokey Pokey at a vacated gate.
- Practice yoga, and invent a few new poses of your own like "downward-facing suitcase" or "flying monkey."
- Have your child work on one of the "Travel Art" projects in this book (beginning on pg. 67).
- Shop for postcards and let your child send greetings to loved ones, even if this means loving scribbles or doodles by his own hand. You can always ask what he'd like you to write for him, too—the answers may surprise you!

On the Go

- Make newspaper hats with abandoned or recycled newspapers (see pg. 65).
- Read a story, or take turns with your child telling your own adventure story so far.

What I've learned: *There are, believe it or not, ways that increasing your numbers actually eases family travel.*

ENTERTAINING TODDLERS ON AIRPLANES

Here are a few creative ways you can entertain children on the airplane before it even takes flight. Hit up your flight attendant for some extra airline napkins, and let the games begin.

- **Have a cleaning party at your seats** with your travel-size antibacterial hand wipes. Many small children love to be "a party" to scrubbing and wiping, and the physical activity, even as your child stays at her own seat, will be very helpful for your prolonged day of travel. Better still, you'll have the added benefit of freshly sanitized airplane trays, arm rests, and seatbelt latches.

- **Fold a stack of airline-issue cocktail napkins together to create a book,** and use a pen to create an all-new story authored by your child. You might tell the adventure of your child's traveling stuffed animal, where you'd be going if the airplane could travel to outer space, or what he thinks the TSA really sees as they X-ray carry-on bags passing through the scanner.

- **Look through the passenger safety brochure** to assign names to the various characters within. Let your child help tell their story of the mommies and daddies discovering the big, big boat slide.

On the Go

- **Turn your air sickness bags (a.k.a. vomit sacks) into hand puppets**. Don't be afraid to use your travel-size cosmetics to really bring them to life. Shredded napkins make great hair, and twisted napkins become the horns of a cow. If your backseat neighbors are not completely terrified by the suggestion and could use a break from the boredom themselves, give them a puppet show over the tops of your seats.

- **Go on a "baby hunt."** If your toddler starts to get antsy after you've reached cruising altitude, go for a stroll to look for babies on the airplane. (Just please don't wake a sleeping baby!)

- **Find another child of similar age** on your flight and offer to trade books or a toy during the journey.

- **Create cocktail napkin origami.** Paper hats are easiest to learn and remember how to make, and may be just the right size for some of your child's travel-size stuffed animals to wear. Decorate the hats with crayons or, in a pinch, ask a neighbor to borrow a pen (instructions follow).

CREATING ORIGAMI HATS FROM NAPKINS

Origami hats are easy to make from napkins, as well as sheets of newspaper or hotel stationery. Ideally you will start with a rectangular-shaped piece of paper, though you can easily adapt a standard airline-issue square cocktail napkin as shown here.

Unfold your napkin into one large square.

Fold the side in about 1 inch to create a rectangle.

Fold the top down to meet the bottom edge.

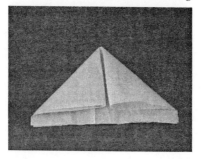

Fold the top two corners down toward the center.

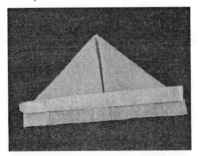

Fold the bottom edge up to create the hat brim, then turn over and repeat with the remaining edge.

TRAVEL CRAFTS FOR PRESCHOOLERS

- Build a pyramid from half-and-half containers at a fast food restaurant or diner. Stacked upside-down works best.

- Make a "book of napkins" and draw scenes from your trip (or your anticipated adventures).

- Use foil gum wrappers to create tiny dishes or a "tea set." Peel the foil from the paper for best results.

- Create rubbings of textures found in your surroundings—tile surface patterns, a coaster, leaves, sidewalk cement, luggage tags—using a peeled crayon or pencil.

On the Go

- Create a two-dimensional (flat) log cabin out of wooden stir sticks collected from a café. Keep the stir sticks in your diaper bag to reuse as needed.

A two-dimensional log cabin created from ten wooden stir sticks collected from a café.

TRAVEL SKETCHES

Date: **Artist:**

Here is a picture of me on vacation.

Date: **Artist:**

Here is a picture of my suitcase.

Date: **Artist:**

Here is a picture of my favorite toy I brought.

Date: **Artist:**

Here is a picture of my favorite place to visit.

Date: **Artist:**

Here is a picture of someone I will visit.

Date: **Artist:**

Here is what I like best about vacations.

WHILE YOU'RE THERE

At Your Accommodations

*When all else fails in the hotel room, unplug the phone
and let him call room service to his heart's content.*

CHECKING-IN SAFETY CHECKLIST

Entering in upon new territory, furnishings, electronics, and décor, your weary little traveler may transform into a whirlwind of terror. Depending on the age and temperament of your child, it may be wise to leave her seated and buckled in the stroller or let her explore the lobby or grounds with your mate while you do your initial safety sweep. Here's what to watch out for:

- **Door locks** – Can you latch the main door to ensure your child won't go sightseeing without you? Does the bathroom or any other room have locks within your child's reach? Be sure to use a chain lock or other upper locks on exterior doors to keep your child from opening them. For interior doors, use your finger guards or door knob covers if you have brought them along[3]. You can also use a rolled-up towel placed over the top of an interior door to keep it from closing.

- **Low/large windows** – Are the windows low enough for the child to run into, or climb out of, or access by climbing on other furniture in the room? Do they open wide enough that toys—or a child—might fall through (remember, screens will not stop children from falling)? Can they be

---

[3] For more help addressing safety concerns as you travel, see Chapter 10 in *Travels with Baby*.

locked shut so your child cannot open them? Is there a "protective" rail or grillwork outside the window that might tempt the child if it is opened for fresh air? Move any furniture your child can climb or will possibly be jumping on (beds!) away from the window, including tables. Be careful easily climbable suitcases don't end up filling in their spaces.

- **Patio doors** – Can your child unlatch or operate the door unassisted? Is the glass so wide it is a walk-through risk? Is the glass so thin or old it might break if bumped by a toy or gallivanting child? Ask your hotel for a different room with a more securely locking patio door if possible (some might be better than others). Keep sheers drawn across thin glass while your child is active, and establish a play area in the room that's a safe distance from that area.

- **Balconies or decks** – Are the railing balusters close enough to keep curious children and babies from slipping under or through? Even more modern hotel buildings may still have railings spaced too widely for small children and babies (remember toddlers are much narrower turned sideways). Be sure to inspect the deck for yourself *before* your child comes out exploring. Never allow the child out on the deck without an adult in close supervision, and be sure that any furniture is moved a safe distance away from the railings. If the railings are simply spaced too wide, request a room on the ground floor if there are patios you might be able to get more use from. Otherwise, use your stroller as a 5-point-safety lounger for your child when you all spend time on the deck.

- **Curtains, blinds, and window treatments** – Give draperies a friendly tug before your child does to ensure they're securely anchored. Get loose operating cords, delicate drapes, and unsafe window treatments up and out of the way, bundled with a rubber band if needed.

- **Heating/AC** – Is the heating or AC unit accessible to your child? Could it be dangerously hot or pose a risk from the operating fan? Are the controls within his reach? Be discreet when changing settings on the unit, and don't be afraid to rearrange furniture or use suitcases to deemphasize the fascinating focal point and perhaps block access to it.

- **Electrical appliances, outlets, and cords** – Watch out for coffeemakers, alarm clocks, and hairdryers that may be pulled off of surfaces by curious toddlers, either by their cords or the objects themselves. Lamp, TV, and Internet cables and cords may also need attention. Outlets may appear where not expected, such as at the base of lamps on desks or bedside tables.

- **Kitchens or kitchenettes** – Check cupboards and drawers for knives, coffeemakers with glass carafes, and other hazards that may be within reach, including matches if the stove is gas. Dish

79

washing detergent and/or cleaning supplies may be kept in an accessible cupboard. Go ahead and relocate items to upper cupboards or onto the countertop. Be aware that ovens, refrigerators, or dishwashers may be more easily opened than yours at home. If they are newer, you can ask the staff for instructions on using the child lock feature on microwaves and dishwashers.

• **Bathrooms** – Soaps, shampoos, and lotions may need to be moved from within reach. In vacation rentals and exchange homes, check for cleaning supplies, medicines, matches, and other hazardous products that may be stored in easily accessible bathroom cabinets, and relocate if necessary. Be sure to store your own toiletries and travel kits out of reach of your child. Those with built-in hooks or loops can be hung from robe hooks, or from shower or closet rods.

• **Minibars** – Can your child open the minibar by herself? Are there items inside that could pose a danger (glass bottles, peanuts or other allergens in snacks, etc.) or could set you back more than you had planned for this vacation? You may need to set a suitcase in front of it or rearrange furniture.

SLEEPING IN NEW SURROUNDINGS

- **Offer some cereal or a whole grain snack** before bedtime to help ensure a good night's rest (see more on pg. 83).

- **Observe a family bedtime** when sharing a single room, tent, or compartment, even if it only lasts until your child is sound asleep in her new bed.

- **Set the hotel's radio alarm clock** to static to help create white noise (call it "waves" if that helps) to help muffle out troublesome street or hotel noise.

- **Ask the front desk for a nightlight** if you forgot yours. Many hotels will have a spare for you to borrow.

- **Block out bright lights**—including ridiculously late hours of sunlight—by hanging an extra blanket or your bedspread over the window. Ask the hotel for an extra blanket if needed.

- **Place the shirt you wore** during the day next to your child's pillow for your familiar and calming scent through the night.

While You're There

CO-SLEEPING FOR NON-CO-SLEEPERS

If you're not accustomed to co-sleeping at home, but suddenly need to share a bed during your travels, it can be a bit of an adjustment for some parents—and some kids. Try these tips.

- **Create a "safe zone" for infants and babies** at the head of the bed, between adult pillows, where blankets and adult elbows won't interfere. Always be certain the child cannot slip between mattresses (as when two twin beds are pushed together) or between the mattress and the wall.

- **When sharing the bed with an excitable tot** (who might be thrilled to play with your hair all night), try putting him to bed first as per your usual routine and waiting until he's soundly asleep before tucking in along side of him. You may need to read stories a bit longer than usual, and don't be afraid to switch to the newspaper if need be.

- **Determine whether or not you can move the bed against a wall on one side**—and if it will stay securely in place. Even if you are the one sleeping against the wall, it may free up some additional space on the mattress.

CONQUERING JETLAG

- **Don't deprive an overtired child of a nap when she needs one, but try to limit the length** of the nap to what is normal at home.

- **Embrace "sleepytime snacks"** containing the natural sleep-aid tryptophan. Try to keep some dry cereal or whole grain snacks on hand for bed time—and possibly midnight snacks.

- **Respect digestion.** As with traveling adults, children may need a few days to alter their elimination clocks to the new time zone as well. He may just need to "play until he's pooped."

- **If your child wakes up with a burst of energy in the middle of the night,** be prepared to roll with it. Most often fatigue will return after an hour's playdate with Mom or Dad (plan ahead to take turns). Encourage calming activities like reading books, bathing, or coloring.

- **Say, "Goodnight Moon"—outside.** For some children, a little fresh air and proof that the world around them is still sleeping can help get them back on track.

What I've learned: There are worse ways to pass the wee hours of night than by pushing a stroller several laps around a glowing swimming pool to the sounds of crickets chirping beneath a starry island sky.

While You're There

ROMANCE REVIVAL TIPS FOR PARENTS

Two double beds packed into a single room with a
Pack 'N Play parked in the corner and any number
of children in your charge does not always set the
mood for romance. Nevertheless, this is your
vacation and, with any luck, you should be able to
enjoy it to the fullest. What are parents to do?

- **Ask about a King room** if your child will be
  sleeping in a portacrib and you have no need for
  additional beds. King rooms generally have
  more space, and king beds are generally more
  romantic.

- **Use any available alcove or niche for your
  child's portacrib** or travel bed. If your room has
  a slightly separated sink area, kitchenette, or
  dressing area, these may be good options.

- **Take advantage of your child's "stroller nap"**
  by strolling her back to your room and parking
  the stroller in a quiet corner of the room (or
  perhaps bathroom).

- **Buy a bottle of wine** and enjoy a glass together
  after your child goes to sleep.

- **Order room service** and enjoy a relaxing dinner
  (or just dessert) in your room after baby calls it a
  night.

- **Ask about an upgrade to a one-bedroom suite**
  as you check in to your hotel. Often the basic

rooms fill up first, and the staff may able to make you a last-minute deal on a larger suite.

- **Use the bedroom of a one-bedroom suite as your children's sleeping quarters** and save the rest of the suite for yourselves. With the kids tucked into their own quiet room, you can enjoy that late-night room service, a movie, foot massages, and the full range of options the rest of your room presents. You can always tip-toe into your bedroom later on, or sleep on the sofa bed.

- **Take advantage of your balcony, deck, or patio** as an extra space to relax together and reminisce while your child takes a nap indoors.

- **Enjoy a bubble bath.** This can be a great way to wind down after a busy vacation day with tots, whether you take a relaxing hot bath while your partner takes care of bedtime stories, or you take a hot bath together after your child goes to sleep.

- **Book a babysitter.** When all else fails, consider hiring a pro to look after your little one if only for a couple of hours while you (sigh) enjoy a meal so quiet you can hear yourself chew, make a relaxing visit to the resort spa, or take a walk on the beach holding hands—grown-up hands. (Tips for hiring local babysitters on pg. 86.)

While You're There

HIRING A LOCAL BABYSITTER

Many hotels and resorts can provide guests with a list of local babysitters on request. If your hotel can provide a list of sitters with references who have served at the hotel in the past without complaint, this may be your simplest solution.

Online sources for babysitters throughout the U.S.

You can also search for caregivers available on short notice in major cities across the U.S. (a registration fee may apply) at these sites:

- www.Care.com
- www.Care4Hire.com
- www.Sittercity.com

Sources for babysitters in some other major international cities

- **Sydney, Australia – Careforkids.com.au** is similar to the U.S.-based agencies above. Register and search babysitters online at www.Careforkids.com.au

- **London, England – Royal Nannies** can help you book a babysitter or nanny with a one-time booking fee (from 10 £). More info at www.nannieslondon.co.uk. You must call to book: +44 (0) 20 7147 9945.

- **Paris, France – Mababysitter Paris** can arrange a babysitter for you at your hotel or vacation rental and will take care of the legal paperwork required in France on your behalf. Info at <u>www.mababysitter.fr</u>.

- **Tokyo, Japan – Japan Baby Sitter Service** has placed nannies and babysitters since the 1970s. Babysitters must be booked by 5 p.m. the day before service is needed. Web site is in Japanese only: <u>www.jbs-mom.co.jp</u>. Call 03-3423-1251.

For help finding babysitting services at additional destinations, visit the planning section at <u>www.TravelswithBaby.com</u>.

CHECKING-OUT CHECKLIST

When you travel with young children, it's especially helpful to recognize that checking out of your vacation accommodations is more than simply re-packing suitcases. This checklist will help streamline the process.

- Get extra cash if needed for the trip home.

- Purchase snacks and drinks if they'll be needed en route.

While You're There

- Re-stock supply of wipes and diapers in diaper bag or carry-on.

- Replace back-up clothing in your diaper bag or carry-on if needed.

- Swap out travel toys and books for a fresh selection for the journey home.

- Remove childproofing products and nightlights.

- Remove any of your child's blankets or bedding you've used in the hotel's crib.

- Prepare any rented baby gear for return per the agency's instructions.

- Check the in-room safe for valuables or travel documents.

- Check the shower and bath for personal items.

- Check the areas where you have used or recharged cameras, PDAs, or a laptop for overlooked personal electronics, cords, and convertors.

- Check under beds for clothing, toys, and other personal items.

- Also check all accessible drawers and cabinets — even those you don't think have been used — for unexpectedly relocated items.

Eating & Feeding

Chances are your child will enjoy many snacks in his travel stroller, but none so much as that first chocolate ice cream cone. Good thing you travel with baby wipes.

BREASTFEEDING ON THE GO

- **Strategically place your child's stroller or diaper bag** to create a privacy barrier while you are out and about.

- **Use a small receiving blanket with one corner tucked under your bra strap** to drape over your child's cheek for privacy. When he's finished nursing, it's ready to double as a burp cloth on your shoulder.

- **Use your sling or child carrier to help position your baby and provide privacy** while nursing. Even while sitting down, this can help save your back and prevent strain on your neck when other support isn't available.

- **When dining out, drape a napkin** over your child's cheek to help give privacy while nursing.

- **While your baby is still very small, use the diaper bag or a folded jacket on your lap** to help keep from hunching over, and use arm rests where you can find them. (In airplanes and cars you may be able to use a pillow.)

- **Sit with your back to the restaurant crowd** for optimal privacy. Trade seats if needed.

DINING OUT WITH BABIES

- **Don't waste your baby's limited patience waiting at an empty table.** Let one parent explore the restaurant with her or even stroll around the block together while you wait for the food to come.

- **For babies not old enough to sit up,** turn square wooden "restaurant-issue" highchairs upside down to use as a base for infant car seats.

- **For babies not big enough to sit comfortably in restaurant highchairs,** wedge your diaper bag, purse, or a folded jacket behind your child for back support.

- **Where highchairs are not available,** be prepared to use your stroller, or use a spare adult-size long-sleeve T-shirt from your suitcase to help secure your baby to the restaurant chair by wrapping the shirt under her arms and tying the sleeves behind the chair (do not leave your child unattended!).

- **Ask for a mug of hot water** to help warm your own bottle at the table.

- **When dinner time comes at the witching hour,** stroll the baby to sleep in her stroller before asking for a corner table or one that is off a main path through the restaurant.

- **When dining with a sleeping baby, look for a bustling restaurant** where the noise level will be somewhat consistent, muffling the clatter of dishes and individual conversations.

DINING OUT WITH TODDLERS

- **Collect a few spare plastic spoons at restaurants where** you find them to give your child at later restaurants where far noisier and more destructive metal spoons are the only option.

- **Never hesitate to ask for an extra plate or bowl** to help simplify sharing food with your child and stretch your food budget farther.

- **Make a "quick-cut straw"** to help your child have better control when the straw is much taller than the child-size cup. Instructions follow on pg. 94.

- **Remember these great side orders to split** among family: rice, mashed potatoes, steamed veggies, French fries.

- **Practice napkin origami** to help pass the time until your order arrives at the table (see pg 65). Make a hat and let your child decorate it with crayons or a pen from your purse.

- **Ask for ice or use some from your water glass** to help preserve leftover milk in sippy cups for continued use outside of the restaurant, and to help cool soup and oatmeal for your hungry tot before he loses patience.

- **Request tables off the beaten path** to help avoid feelings of "spilt guilt" from everyone having to step over food debris in their path.

- **Fill your child first** when you know you'll be dining later at a restaurant or event where he won't care for the menu, or past his natural dinner time. With a full tummy, you can let him stay busy with a toy or activity at the table as you enjoy your meal.

- **Get it to go** when you'd rather give your child his favorites at the hotel room and be able to enjoy your meal while he plays or watches a DVD. Many restaurants are happy to accommodate with take-out orders even if they don't advertise it.

- **Tip generously** when leaving food on the floor (and possibly other parts) of a restaurant and you can leave knowing that your good traveler's karma is still intact.

While You're There

Bend the straw where you would like it to end.

Next, use a table knife to pull against the fold and cut through the straw.

Put the freshly cut end of the straw down in the cup as it may be slightly rough.

EASY BREAKFASTS FOR THE HOTEL ROOM

- **Instant oatmeal** – Simply heat water in your hotel room coffeemaker to add to the oatmeal. If you don't have kid-proof bowls from home, use the ceramic mugs or thick glasses in your room (and plastic spoons from a café you've passed along the way). Add raisins, other dried fruit, crumbled nuts for protein, or a handful of granola to spruce it up. I sometimes bring a baggie with vanilla protein powder from home to stir in as well (and ground flax meal, but don't tell the kids).

- **Fruit** – Pick up some bananas, oranges, apples or other seasonal fruit that can keep in your room without refrigeration or special preparation. Just be sure you follow the rules if you're where water safety is an issue: "Boil it, cook it, peel it, or forget it!" (See more food safety tips, pg. 96)

- **Bagels** – You may prefer them lightly toasted and smothered with cream cheese, but in a pinch "soft bagels" can provide a decent starter course for your day—our favorite bagged brand dishes out 12g of protein per bagel!

- **Peanut butter and crackers** – A small jar of peanut butter that requires no refrigeration after opening (look to the megabrands) can give the whole family that early morning protein it needs for a strong, energetic start. Paired with your child's favorite crackers—voilà! Also makes a great pick-me-up snack in the afternoon.

- **Protein-packed breakfast cereal** – Cereal may seem like a no-brainer here, but the box you choose can have everything to do with your family having a good (or the other kind of) morning. Check the labels to ensure you'll be getting as much protein per serving as possible, or pair your breakfast bowl with a protein-rich food (more on pg. 83).

- **Apple sauce cups** – Shelf-stable, single-serving apple sauces require no refrigeration and come ready to serve in their own bowls.

FOOD AND WATER SAFETY TIPS

If you're traveling in an area where food and water safety is a real concern, it's critically important to protect your child, whose immature digestive and immune systems are especially vulnerable. As your child's caregiver, you'll want to make sure you eat and drink responsibly, too. Caring for young children while suffering from Montezuma's revenge is no way to spend a vacation!

- **Bathe children with care.** If the tap water is not considered safe for drinking at your destination, make sure to keep bath and shower water out of your children's mouths as well. Explain to preschoolers that, just as it's important not to swallow the tap water from a cup, they should also avoid swallowing any of it from the tub.

- **Drink sealed, bottled water and beverages.** If you don't recognize the brand of bottled water, check the label for "IBWA" (International Bottled Water Association) or "NSF" (National Sanitation Foundation) certification.

- **Pass on the ice.** Freezing water does not kill the harmful microbes that may be in it, and outside of some very large resorts, few establishments actually make ice from bottled water.

- **Wash and sterilize with care.** Although the tap water in North American cities is now considered safe enough for washing infants' bottles, it would be prudent to raise your standards while traveling abroad. If the water is not considered drinkable where you stay, do not use it untreated for washing bottles and nipples, nor sippy cups, reusable water bottles, and the like. Since air-drying does not necessarily kill the bad critters, use bottled or boiled water instead. The same care should be taken with teething toys, pacifiers, or other items that go into your child's mouth.

While You're There

- **Bring it to a boil.** If you need to boil water for safe consumption, the rule of thumb is to let it boil for one full minute, or for three minutes at high elevations (over 6,562 feet or 2,000 meters). Boiling drinking water for an extended period of time is not recommended as it can increase the concentration of lead in the water.

- **Avoid food from street vendors.** As friendly and generous as they may be, they often have little or no refrigeration available for the foods they prepare and likely do not have a place to wash their hands with clean water or soap.

- **Seek out restaurants frequented and recommended by many Western travelers.** They are more accustomed to satisfying Western stomachs and standards, and if they don't, you will likely hear about it.

- **Wash the hand that feeds you!** All of these precautions will do little good if you don't wash your hands or those of your child before snacks or meals. Keep antibacterial hand wipes in your day pack and use them—especially for children whose hands frequently find their way into their mouths (mealtime or not).

Health & Medical Help

What I've learned: *A medic can tell a 1-year-old to keep her bandage clean and dry—and on—during the rest of her vacation in Mexico, but I've found waterproof first-aid tape (and lots of it) to be far more effective.*

FINDING A LOCAL DOCTOR OR DENTIST

- **Contact your doctor's office at home** in case they have a referral in the area (see your Emergency Contacts, pg. 139).
- **If you are staying at a hotel,** the front desk may have doctor referrals and information on local drop-in clinics where travelers may be helped.
- **In the U.S. and Canada,** try The American Academy of Pediatrics' online directory, which lists pediatricians and pediatric dentists in both countries, all of whom are members of the American Academy of Pediatrics: www.aap.org/referral.
- **Where English-speaking or Western-trained doctors may be difficult to find**, the International Association for Medical Assistance to Travellers (IAMAT) can help you find a doctor if needed, and at pre-set prices. It is best to join the organization and get your membership card and packet *before* you travel, but in a pinch, try them at www.iamat.org or email info@iamat.org. Membership is free, but a donation to the organization is encouraged.

HELP FOR COMMON AILMENTS

Cough and Congestion

- If the air is particularly dry where you're staying, run a hot steamy shower to help humidify the air.

- Croupy cough (song of the barking seal) is often helped by stepping outside into cool night air.

- Use the saline nasal drops from your child's Travel Kit (as recommended in *Travels with Baby*) to help moisten nasal passages and loosen up congestion.

- Moisten a washcloth with hot water and hold near your child's nose. When it's cool enough, gently rub the nose to help loosen debris.

- Vapor plugs that simply plug into standard electrical outlets (like air fresheners) can also be used to release aromatic oils of menthol, eucalyptus, etc., into the air to ease congestion. Brands include SudaCare and Pediacare, and may be available at the local pharmacy or supermarket.

- Vicks BabyRub and other brands of "baby chest rub" can also be massaged on the chest and neck to help clear congestion and sooth dry passages for babies 3 months and older (should be in your child's Travel Kit).

- If bad congestion is preventing your child from sleeping, consider using your semi-reclined travel stroller to help keep your child's head elevated while she rests. As always, make sure she's securely buckled and don't leave her unattended.

Dehydration

Approximately 50% of an adult's body weight is water, but a baby's weight is more than 75% water. That's why babies and young children can become dehydrated far more quickly than adults, so it's especially important to keep the fluids flowing to them and through them as you travel. To help prevent dehydration[4]:

- Breastfeed on demand

- Keep water bottles handy for everyone

- Take frequent "water breaks"

- Offer popsicles

- Dilute juice with extra water

---

[4] Note: Gatorade and adult sports drinks are not recommended for babies or young children.

- Limit exposure to sun and wind, especially for babies

Heat, sun, high altitudes, and wind exposure can all increase the risk of dehydration, as can illness accompanied by vomiting and diarrhea. Breastfeeding mothers must be extra careful to stay hydrated enough for themselves and their babies who depend on their milk.

If you think your child may be at risk for dehydration, watch out for the following warning signs:

- Fewer than six wet diapers in a day
- No tears when baby or child cries
- Dark urine
- Sunken eyes
- Wrinkled-looking skin

If increasing your child's fluid intake doesn't seem to be helping, or illness is causing dehydration to worsen, be sure to contact a doctor right away (see pg. 100 for help finding a local doctor).

Diarrhea or loose stools

Diarrhea is one of the most common ailments children may experience during travel, primarily because their inexperienced immune systems are more likely to succumb to food- and waterborne

103

While You're There

illnesses encountered through eating or merely from their frequent and indiscriminant hand-to-mouth contact (or even toys or pacifiers touching the floor). Watch closely for symptoms of dehydration (see pg. 102) as it is the greatest risk associated with diarrhea in babies and small children. The CDC advises immediate medical attention for infants and small children with the following symptoms.

Seek immediate medical help when diarrhea is accompanied by:

- Signs of moderate to severe dehydration
- Blood in the stool
- A fever greater than 101.5 F
- Persistent vomiting

Milder cases of diarrhea or unpleasantly loose stools may be improved by eating these popular toddler foods we affectionately call "hinder binders," or you might remember them best as "The Firm Five":

The Firm Five

- Cheerios
- Bananas
- Applesauce
- Cheese
- Yogurt

Constipation

Constipation can affect children for many reasons while traveling, including a refusal to eat new and unfamiliar foods that may be necessary to maintain a balanced diet or, for potty-trained or –training children, a fear of using new facilities. If you suspect diet is the cause of the constipation, try to reduce the constipating foods in the diet, including The Firm Five listed above, and replace them with more high-fiber options. If fruits and vegetables are refused, remember these alternatives can also work wonders. Note: high fiber foods should always be consumed with plenty of fluids.

High-fiber foods for picky eaters

- Beans (baked beans, kidney, pinto, etc.)
- Sweet potatoes
- Peas
- Popcorn
- Graham crackers
- Whole wheat bread

While You're There

A TRAVELER'S GUIDE TO EAR INFECTIONS

Just the thought of a possible ear infection during travel is enough to keep some parents from ever leaving home. It is hard to see a child in pain, it is hard to soothe a child in pain, it is hard to sleep with a child in pain, and it is sometimes impossible to tell on your own what the pain is even from. The question, "Is it an ear infection?" sends countless parents to the pediatrician's office each year, many getting assured that it's probably just teething.

Yet FamilyDoctor.org reports that more than three out of four children will have at least one ear infection before the age of three. So what do you do if you suspect that one of those children is yours—and you're nowhere near your pediatrician's office? First, stay calm. Monitor your child's symptoms. If she is not old enough to tell you, "I have acute pain in my middle ear," or something to that effect, consider the following:

It's less likely to be an ear infection if your child...

- Has not recently had a cold. Ear infections generally begin when "germs" from the illness travel up the eustachian tube.
- Has no fever or a low fever of less than 101° F (could be teething).
- Meets the above criteria and becomes more like herself after a dose of acetaminophen or ibuprofen.

It's more likely to be an ear infection if your child...

- Has been fighting a cold that has produced yellow or greenish mucus.
- Has a fever of 101° F or more.
- Cries or fusses more in a reclined position than when sitting up.
- Has pus or bloody discharge coming from the ear (pus without fever could indicate swimmer's ear).

If your child's symptoms point toward an ear infection, and you have seen no discharge or pus, you can begin treating the pain immediately with Similasan Earache Relief drops, which are available over the counter at most pharmacies (good to have in your suitcase if your child is prone to ear infections). You may also give the correct dosage of either ibuprofen or acetaminophen (Dr. Sears advises that you can safely use both ibuprofen and acetaminophen together if one alone is not enough), and apply a warm compress to her ears, or warm washcloth, or water bottle filled with warm water.

Continue to monitor and alleviate your child's symptoms, as you are able. If they persist, you can proceed to find a local doctor in the morning. And it may be helpful, possibly even reassuring, to understand a little more about ear infections and their treatment.

Here are answers to traveling parents' top questions about ear infections:

Q: What if we can't see a doctor—or get antibiotics—right away?

Keep in mind that ear infections may be the result of either bacteria or a virus reaching the inner ear—and since antibiotics cannot treat viruses, they simply will have no effect on some ear infections, though they are often prescribed regardless.

Recent studies have also shown that 80% of ear infections will clear up on their own in less than a week without antibiotics. In fact, the American Academy of Family Physicians and the American Academy of Pediatrics now recommend a treatment approach that emphasizes observation and pain relief before using antibiotics.

However, on occasion, complications can occur, and if antibiotics can help your child begin to feel better and recover more quickly (which they most likely will if it is a bacterial infection), that is worth a lot—especially when traveling!

So the bottom line is, don't panic if you can't get to a doctor immediately when you suspect an ear infection, but by all means do what you can to help your child feel better until you can get there.

108

Q: Does the drainage from the ear mean the eardrum has ruptured?

Pus or bloody drainage from the ear can be alarming and, in the case of an ear infection, usually means the eardrum has ruptured. This is not as devastating as it sounds, however, and it usually results in an immediate feeling of relief for the child. The ruptured eardrum is usually treated with antibiotic eardrops prescribed by your child's physician.

Q: Should we delay the flight?

If your child is indeed diagnosed with an ear infection, it could be a good idea to delay flying until the infection has passed, if possible. Extra fluids built up in the ears can make it even more difficult for the pressure to equalize in a child's already narrow eustachian tubes. Discuss the type of ear infection and stage that it's at with the doctor and tell her when your flight is currently scheduled. If possible, bring some pain reliever (e.g., Infants' or Children's Tylenol) and Similasan Earache Relief drops onboard when you do fly, just in case there is any lingering discomfort. Both Infants' Tylenol or infants' ibuprofen and Similisan drops are available in sizes appropriate for your liquid allowance for carry-on.

While You're There

BREASTFEEDING PROBLEMS & SOLUTIONS

While breastfeeding can greatly simplify travel with babies and provide numerous benefits to traveling babies, interrupted—and augmented—feeding schedules and hygienic challenges can make breastfeeding moms more vulnerable to certain issues during travel. Here are tips to help avoid them, and help in case you don't.

Engorgement – Spend a night in the tent trying to keep baby happy and the campground from waking, or surviving a similar scenario on the red-eye to Miami, and you might spend your next day watching baby snooze and blissfully catch up on her zzz's while you sport an extra cup size or two and the discomfort that goes with it.

If so, make sure you wear loose-fitting clothing, as tight clothing may not only aggravate the condition, but could also make you more prone to mastitis. Consider trading in the nursing bra for a camisole, tank, or sundress for the day. If you have a pump with you, use it. Otherwise, you may get some relief from a warm shower and hand-expressing some milk. You can also encourage a make-up feeding in place of a snack.

Mastitis – This type of breast infection, characterized by acute pain and often flu-like symptoms, is caused by bacteria somehow crossing paths with the nipple area. Though it can be a challenge to keep your hands clean during travel, this is an especially good reason to keep antibacterial hand wipes with you for times you can't wash hands between a diaper change—or a trip through the train station—and a feeding. Considering the close contact of your child's hands to the breast during feedings, it's a good idea to give those a cleansing swipe before feedings as well.

Antibiotics are usually prescribed to help clear up the infection (see pg. 100 for help finding a local doctor if needed). If you can't get to a doctor right away, continue nursing from the affected breast. Though painful, emptying the breast and allowing it to refill with fresh milk is one of its best defenses during infection. For immediate relief, consider taking a pain reliever/fever reducer and fill the plastic laundry bag provided by your hotel or the liner from a champagne bucket with ice to use as a cold compress.

Sore Nipples – Whether you've been breastfeeding an overtired child much more than usual or she is becoming so distracted by other passengers in the aircraft or the excitement of the train that she no longer latches properly, sore nipples must be given the respect and care they deserve.

Insist on a proper latch and take your child off the breast and start over when it's anything less. You might also find some relief by trying a different nursing position, such as the football hold. To give relief to dry or cracked nipples, use a lanolin-based nipple ointment such as Lansinoh that will be water-resistant and safe for baby. If the pain is accompanied by any of the symptoms of candida, see the next point.

Yeast Infection or Candida – Long flights in a stuffy airplane with a snug nursing bra and moist breast pads is a pretty ideal set-up for a painful yeast infection of the nipples. If you are suddenly experiencing shooting pains in the nipple during feedings, have blisters on the nipple area, and/or have recently finished a course of antibiotics, yeast may be a likely culprit.

While sunshine and fresh air are two of the best remedies for this "fungal" condition, checking into a nudist resort for the remainder of your vacation may not be an option. Instead, wear loose-fitting clothing in breathable fabrics, and leave the bra in the carry-on while you rest on that next red-eye. Try to keep your nipples dry as much as possible, and wash bras and breast pads in hot water to help prevent reinfection.

Eating yogurt with live and active cultures or taking probiotics (available at most health stores) may also help your system fight the fungus. Note that it is possible to develop a yeast infection of the nipple whether or not your baby shows signs of candida at the mouth area, also called "thrush" (typically a whitish tongue and minute cottage cheese-like bumps are the giveaway).

If your child does show signs of thrush, however, or your own infection does not respond quickly to improved conditions, consult a physician who can prescribe the appropriate medication (see pg. 100 for help finding a local doctor if needed). In some countries, the pharmacist will be able to provide you with the appropriate medicine after a consultation.

BREASTFEEDING RESOURCES

In case you need help addressing any of these or other breastfeeding issues while away from home, these organizations can provide you with breastfeeding information and support.

- **La Leche League International** – The website includes local contact information for many chapters found around the world. Visit http://www.lalecheleague.org online or call 1-800-LALECHE.

- **International Lactation Consultant Assoc. (ILCA)** – Find an International Board Certified Lactation Consultant in destinations across the U.S. and around the world. Visit www.ilca.org or call 1-919-861-5577.

While You're There

If you have Internet access, the following sites offer helpful sections on breastfeeding problems and advice:

- **Ask Dr. Sears** – www.askdrsears.com

- **Baby Center**– www.babycenter.com

- **About.com** – http://pediatrics.about.com

Staying Abroad

What I've learned: *Not everyone in the world thinks diapers belong beside their next dinner. In France, I had no trouble finding baby food as I shopped in smaller markets, but diapers continued to elude me until someone explained I needed to purchase them at the pharmacy.*

While You're There

BABYTALK IN FOUR LANGUAGES

English →	Spanish
baby	bebé
child	niño[5]
diapers/nappies	pañales
infant formula	leche para infantes
warm milk	leche caliente
cold milk	leche fría
baby food	alimento para bebé
baby bottle	biberón
crib/cot	cuna
highchair	trona alta
stroller/buggy	cochecito

English →	French
baby	bébé
child	enfant
diapers/nappies	couches

---

[5] *Niño* is used for baby in general, but your daughter specifically will be the feminine *niña*.

116

(English →	French, continued)
infant formula	lait en poudre pour bébé
warm milk	lait chaud
cold milk	lait froid
baby food	aliment pour bébés
baby bottle	biberon
crib/cot	lit de bébé
highchair	chaise haute
stroller/buggy	poussette

English →	German
baby	Baby
child	Kind
diapers/nappies	Windeln
infant formula	Säuglingsnahrung
warm milk	warme Milch
cold milk	kalte Milch
baby food	Babynahrung
baby bottle	Babyflasche
crib/cot	Krippe/Kinderbett
highchair	Hochstuhl
stroller/buggy	Kinderwagen

While You're There

English →	Italian
baby	bambino[6]
child	bambino
diapers/nappies	pannolini
infant formula	latte artificiale
warm milk	latte caldo
cold milk	latte freddo
baby food	cibo per bambini
baby bottle	biberon
crib/cot	lettino/culla
highchair	seggiolone
stroller/buggy	passeggino

What I've learned: *Highchairs are not only uncommon to find in restaurants outside of North America, but an effective translation for the word "highchair" doesn't exist in some countries. Be warned that, in some situations, you may raise some eyebrows requesting a bar stool for your baby. See tips for dining without highchairs, pg. 91.*

---

[6] In Italian, a baby is in general a *bambino*, but your daughter specifically will be the feminine *bambina*.

TEMPERATURES: CELSIUS & FAHRENHEIT

0°C	32°F
7° C	45°F
15°C	60°F
24°C	75°F
30°C	85°F
35°C	95°F
40°C	104°F

Normal body temperature: 37°C or 98.6°F

CHILD WEIGHTS: LBS. & KGS.

7 lbs	=	3 kgs
10 lbs	=	4.5 kgs
13 lbs	=	6 kgs
17.5 lbs	=	8 kgs
22 lbs	=	10 kgs
33 lbs	=	15 kgs
44 lbs	=	20 kgs
55 lbs	=	25 kgs

While You're There

67 lbs	=	30 kgs
80 lbs	=	36 kgs

CHILD HEIGHTS: INCHES & CENTIMETERS

18.5″	=	47 cm
22″	=	56 cm
25″	=	63.5 cm
28″	=	71 cm
30″	=	76.2 cm
32″	=	81 cm
35″	=	89 cm
38″	=	96.5 cm
41″	=	104 cm
45″	=	114 cm
48"	=	122 cm

OUR FAMILY'S
TRAVELS

Our Trip Notes

Our family on vacation.

What we've learned:

TRIP 1 DESTINATION:

Dates of travel:

Ticket/reservation confirmation numbers:

Departure/return times:

Taxi or car service phone number:

Address(es) of accommodations:

Traveler's insurance contact & policy number:

Our Family's Travels

Other important details and notes:

My age:

How we got there:

Where we stayed:

Where I slept:

How I slept:

Our Trip Notes

Fun things we did:

My favorite things on this trip:

What I miss from home:

Favorite family moments and quotes:

Notes for next time:

Our Family's Travels

TRIP 2 DESTINATION:

Dates of travel:

Ticket/reservation confirmation numbers:

Departure/return times:

Taxi or car service phone number:

Address(es) of accommodations:

Traveler's insurance contact & policy number:

Other important details and notes:

My age:

How we got there:

Where we stayed:

Where I slept:

How I slept:

Fun things we did:

Our Family's Travels

My favorite things on this trip:

What I miss from home:

Favorite family moments and quotes:

Notes for next time:

TRIP 3 DESTINATION:

Dates of travel:

Ticket/reservation confirmation numbers:

Departure/return times:

Taxi or car service phone number:

Address(es) of accommodations:

Traveler's insurance contact & policy number:

Our Family's Travels

Other important details and notes:

My age:

How we got there:

Where we stayed:

Where I slept:

How I slept:

Our Trip Notes

Fun things we did:

My favorite things on this trip:

What I miss from home:

Favorite family moments and quotes:

Notes for next time:

Our Family's Travels

TRIP 4 DESTINATION:

Dates of travel:

Ticket/reservation confirmation numbers:

Departure/return times:

Taxi or car service phone number:

Address(es) of accommodations:

Traveler's insurance contact & policy number:

Other important details and notes:

My age:

How we got there:

Where we stayed:

Where I slept:

How I slept:

Fun things we did:

Our Family's Travels

My favorite things on this trip:

What I miss from home:

Favorite family moments and quotes:

Notes for next time:

TRIP 5 DESTINATION:

Dates of travel:

Ticket/reservation confirmation numbers:

Departure/return times:

Taxi or car service phone number:

Address(es) of accommodations:

Traveler's insurance contact & policy number:

Other important details and notes:

Our Family's Travels

My age:

How we got there:

Where we stayed:

Where I slept:

How I slept:

Fun things we did:

136

My favorite things on this trip:

What I miss from home:

Favorite family moments and quotes:

Notes for next time:

In Case of Emergency

INTERNATIONAL EMERGENCY PHONE NUMBERS

Travelers visiting foreign countries with a SIM card-enabled cell phone will usually have their emergency number from home automatically rerouted to the local emergency number where they are. Other useful numbers to know follow:

- **Poison Control anywhere in the U.S. 1-800-222-1212**

- **Dial 911 for emergencies in:** United States, Canada, Cayman Islands, Costa Rica, Dominican Republic, El Salvador, Panama

- **Dial 066 for emergencies in:** Mexico (some areas will redirect 911 calls automatically)

- **Dial 112 for emergencies in:** Western European countries

- **Dial 000 for emergencies in:** Australia

- **Dial 111 for emergencies in:** New Zealand

INSURANCE AND MEDICAL CONTACTS

Doctor's name:

Doctor's phone number:

Advice line/email:

Medical insurance plan and group:

Medical insurance policy number:

Additional doctor's name:

Doctor's phone number:

Advice line/email:

Our Family's Travels

Medical insurance plan and group:

Medical insurance policy number:

Dentist's name:

Dentist's phone number:

Dental insurance plan:

Dental insurance policy number:

Auto insurance plan and policy number:

Auto insurance phone number:

Emergency roadside assistance (if other):

EMERGENCY CONTACTS

Contact Name(s):

Phone number:

Mobile:

Email address:

Address:

Contact Name(s):

Phone number:

Mobile:

Email address:

Address:

Our Family's Travels

Contact Name(s):

Phone number:

Mobile:

Email address:

Address:

Contact Name(s):

Phone number:

Mobile:

Email address:

Address:

Helpful Details for Our Family

Driver's license numbers:

Passport numbers:

Mileage plan numbers:

Current medications and dosages:

Current prescriptions and Rx numbers:

Our Family's Travels

Other important details:

Weights & Measurements for (child 1): _____

Date: _____ Weight: _____ lbs./kg. Height: _____ in./cm.

Date: _____ Weight: _____ lbs./kg. Height: _____ in./cm.

Date: _____ Weight: _____ lbs./kg. Height: _____ in./cm.

Date: _____ Weight: _____ lbs./kg. Height: _____ in./cm.

Date: _____ Weight: _____ lbs./kg. Height: _____ in./cm.

Date: _____ Weight: _____ lbs./kg. Height: _____ in./cm.

Date: _____ Weight: _____ lbs./kg. Height: _____ in./cm.

Date: _____ Weight: _____ lbs./kg. Height: _____ in./cm.

Date: _____ Weight: _____ lbs./kg. Height: _____ in./cm.

Date: _____ Weight: _____ lbs./kg. Height: _____ in./cm.

Our Family's Travels

Weights & Measurements for (child 2): _____

Date: _____ Weight: _____ lbs./kg. Height: _____ in./cm.

Date: _____ Weight: _____ lbs./kg. Height: _____ in./cm.

Date: _____ Weight: _____ lbs./kg. Height: _____ in./cm.

Date: _____ Weight: _____ lbs./kg. Height: _____ in./cm.

Date: _____ Weight: _____ lbs./kg. Height: _____ in./cm.

Date: _____ Weight: _____ lbs./kg. Height: _____ in./cm.

Date: _____ Weight: _____ lbs./kg. Height: _____ in./cm.

Date: _____ Weight: _____ lbs./kg. Height: _____ in./cm.

Date: _____ Weight: _____ lbs./kg. Height: _____ in./cm.

Date: _____ Weight: _____ lbs./kg. Height: _____ in./cm.

Index

Start your family's next adventure at

www.TravelswithBaby.com

Stop by and start planning your next great family getaway. Find inspiration, help, and advice in:

- FAQs and popular topics
- Destination tips and ideas
- Family-friendly hotel and vacation rental reviews
- Candid advice and recommendations from "Moms Around the World"
- Baby travel gear reviews and advice
- Worldwide directory of baby gear rental agencies

Help make this a better book

We welcome your feedback and suggestions for future editions of *Take-Along Travels with Baby*. Please address correspondence to Shelly Rivoli, Travels with Baby, Books P.O. Box 7696, Berkeley, CA 94707, or email contact@TravelswithBaby.com.

Get it for your gadget!

Take-Along Travels with Baby is also available for the Amazon Kindle and in Kindle apps for the iPad, iPhone, iPod touch, PC, Mac, Blackberry, and Android devices.

Gold winner in Parenting Resources from the National Parenting Publication Awards (NAPPA)

Finalist for two *ForeWord Magazine* Book of the Year Awards in Travel and Parenting categories

Travels with Baby: The Ultimate Guide for Planning Trips with Babies, Toddlers, and Preschool-Age Children has everything you need to plan enjoyable, safe, and stress-free trips with your child from birth through preschool.

- Plan best-bet trips for your child's changing ages and stages.
- Get tips for planning vacations well-suited to your child's unique temperament.
- Decide what to pack and how to pack it.
- Plan overseas travel with confidence.
- Discover the best cruise lines, airlines, and resorts for families with babies and young children.

Whether you're planning travel by car, plane, train, cruise ship, to the beach, to the woods, or to several other countries, this guide will help you make informed choices and inspired journeys with your family.

About Auth

After changing four continents, baby's double e in Europe, seeki for a toddler combating carsickness in and delicately negotiating a diaper blowout in restaurant in Denver, Shelly Rivoli still traveling with babies and young children i and an honor—and can be lots and lots of fun

Her family travel tips and advice have American Baby, The Boston Globe, LA Ti Magazine, Parenting, Parents, Pregnancy, and York Kids, as well as online at iVill Babble.com. She has also made several appearances on the topic of travel with your

Shelly is the author of the award-winnin with Baby: The Ultimate Guide for Planning T Toddlers, and Preschool-Age Children and th size companion Take-Along Travels with Ba her home in the San Francisco Bay Area w and three young children. For more tips, her latest blog posts, visit www.Trave